·FOOLPROOF·

MICROWAVE

FOOLPROOF

MICROWAVE

60 FUSS-FREE RECIPES TO MAKE THE MOST OF YOUR MICROWAVE
AMY STEPHENSON

PHOTOGRAPHY BY RITA PLATTS

quadrille

Publishing Director
Sarah Lavelle

Commissioning Editor
Stacey Cleworth

Project Editor
Sofie Shearman

Series Designer
Emily Lapworth

Designer
Alicia House

Photographer
Rita Platts

Food Stylist
Amy Stephenson

Prop Stylist
Max Robinson

Head of Production
Stephen Lang

Senior Production Controller
Sabeena Atchia

Quadrille, Penguin Random House UK, One Embassy Gardens, 8 Viaduct Gardens, London SW11 7BW

Quadrille Publishing Limited is part of the Penguin Random House group of companies whose addresses can be found at global.penguinrandomhouse.com

Penguin
Random House
UK

Published by Quadrille in 2024

www.penguin.co.uk

A CIP catalogue record for this book is available from the British Library

ISBN 9781837832309
10 9 8 7 6 5 4 3 2

Colour reproduction by F1

Printed in China by C&C Offset Printing Ltd

The authorised representative in the EEA is Penguin Random House Ireland, Morrison Chambers, 32 Nassau Street, Dublin D02 YH68.

Penguin Random House is committed to a sustainable future for our business, our readers and our planet. This book is made from Forest Stewardship Council® certified paper.

FSC
www.fsc.org
MIX
Paper | Supporting responsible forestry
FSC® C018179

CONTENTS

INTRODUCTION

It's hard to think of a more popular kitchen appliance than the microwave: more than 90 per cent of British households currently own one. And yet they've only existed since the 1940s, when a happy accident led engineer Percy Spencer to discover this radical new way of heating food. Spencer was working on a device called a magnetron, which generates microwaves, when he noticed that a chocolate bar in his pocket had melted. Correctly believing that the vibrations had caused the chocolate to melt, he then tried putting the microwaves into contact with other foods, making popcorn and cooking whole eggs (this needed a little more work), and the microwave was born.

The popularity of microwaves soared during the 1970s as they became more affordable, but this coincided with an increase in the availability of ready meals, which meant that for a long time, microwaves have been associated with unhealthy convenience food.

Today, more and more people are discovering the benefits of cooking from scratch, using a microwave to speed up the process and reduce budgets. At the time of writing, global energy costs are at an all-time high and households are looking to find ways to minimize their energy bills and cook more economically. A microwave typically costs around £30 ($38) per year to run while a gas hob can cost up to £120 ($153). My hope is that this book will provide you with quick and easy recipes that are not only very tasty but will also save you money.

Throughout the book I've shared my top tips for successful microwave cooking: the discoveries I've made as I've created these recipes – toasted nuts, crispy vegetables, buttery soft aubergine and perfectly cooked fish (without the accompanying smell), as well as how to avoid microwave disasters, such as lava-like porridge and exploding eggs (see page 77). My aim is show you how you can make delicious meals from scratch and have your family and friends saying, 'You made *this* in the microwave?!'.

How do microwaves work?

A lot of people typically only use their microwaves to reheat, defrost and melt foods, but there is so much more you can do with them as I hope this book will show.

So what actually is a microwave? Not just the name of the appliance, microwaves are tiny waves of radiation that cause the water, fat and sugar in food to vibrate. This vibration creates heat, which cooks the food. For the process to be safe, the microwaves must be harnessed, which is why they are contained inside a metal box. The same technology is used for MRI scans, aeroplanes and those little pouches you can put your car keys in to protect them from being cloned.

The benefits

- Microwave cooking is generally less smelly than cooking on a hob.

- Microwaves are easy to clean and food doesn't get baked on to dishes as it can in the oven.

- They are cheaper to run than the oven and hob.

- It's harder to overcook things because, unlike the oven and hob, the microwave switches itself off, so you won't burn things as easily.

Top tips

- The best tip I can offer you is to keep checking your food during cooking. You will get to know your own machine and will be able adjust cooking times accordingly.

- Don't try to cook too much at once. I quickly learned that it's not easy cooking huge portions and microwaves are best for one or two servings.

- Before I started writing these recipes I bought a plastic plate cover (from an unnamed Swedish homeware shop) for £1 ($1.30) to cover the food inside the microwave, which is cheaper (and more eco-friendly) than a roll of cling film (plastic wrap) and works very well. Many microwave containers also come with a lid. Just be sure to cover loosely to allow some steam to escape.

- Covering your dish with a plate also works well when the liquid in the food isn't likely to bubble up.

- Milk will bubble up ferociously, so you will need to keep a very keen eye on it during cooking.

Dos & don'ts

DO cook in glass, ceramic and microwave-safe plastic dishes.

DON'T use non-microwave safe plastic or cardboard containers.

DON'T ever put metal, such as cutlery or foil, in the microwave; this is a fire and explosion hazard!

DON'T use a big bowl that only just fits inside your microwave, especially if you are cooking something in liquid. It's hard to get in and out, especially when it's hot, and it can dislodge the plate inside your microwave as it rotates, potentially causing spillages.

A note on power settings

The microwave I used when writing these recipes had a full-power setting of 800W. Unless otherwise stated, all the recipes have been cooked on this power setting. You may need to adjust the timings slightly if your microwave's full power is 700W, 900W or 1000W. Always consult the manufacturer's instruction manual for your microwave before you start cooking to familiarize yourself with its features and attributes. All machines vary.

BREAKFAST

Porridge is probably where your mind goes to when you think of microwaveable breakfasts so I have, of course, included a foolproof recipe, but there are lots more morning treats you can make. Try a banana and maple mug muffin, which is perfect for taking with you on busy mornings, scrambled eggs with bacon, and even poached eggs in a classic eggs Benedict. The best part is that they all cook in under 10 minutes.

PORRIDGE WITH PLUMS, ALMONDS AND MAPLE SYRUP

Porridge is a classic microwave breakfast. This version takes a little longer than the sugar-laden convenience pots available in shops, but it's hopefully worth the effort for the superior texture and flavour.

2 tbsp flaked almonds
75g (3oz) rolled oats
300ml (1¼ cups) milk
2 plums (or peaches or nectarines),
    stoned and sliced
2 tbsp maple syrup
salt

Spread the almonds out in a single layer on a microwaveable plate and microwave on high (800W) for 3 minutes, stirring halfway through and checking them during the last 30 seconds to make sure that they don't burn.

Mix the oats, milk, 100ml (scant ½ cup) of water and a pinch of salt in a microwaveable bowl or jug. Microwave for 2½ minutes, stir, then microwave for 1½ minutes and stir again.

Return to the microwave for a further 1–2 minutes, checking the bowl every 30 seconds to ensure the porridge doesn't boil over.

Divide the porridge between two bowls, top with the sliced fruit, toasted almonds and maple syrup, and serve.

Serves 2
–
Prep 2 mins
–
Cook 9 mins

GRANOLA BARS

This recipe simply uses the microwave to melt ingredients together. It makes for a very speedy breakfast bar to be eaten on the go.

3 tbsp coconut oil
3 tbsp crunchy peanut butter
3 tbsp maple syrup
100g (3½ oz) rolled oats
50g (2oz) mixed nuts or any nut
    of your choice (optional)
30g (1¼oz) mixed seeds
50g (2oz) dried fruit of your choice
    (I use raisins)
¼ tsp ground cinnamon

Place the coconut oil, peanut butter and maple syrup into a large microwaveable bowl and microwave on high (800W) for 45 seconds, stirring halfway through, until everything is melted.

Add the oats, nuts, seeds, dried fruit and cinnamon to the bowl and stir well. Microwave for 1 minute.

Line a small tin with baking parchment (I used a 25 × 18cm/ 10 × 7in tin but similar-sized tins will work just as well – it doesn't need to be exact) and tip the mixture in, pressing it down so that it's flat and even.

Transfer to the fridge and chill for at least 30 minutes, until firm, then cut into 10 pieces. Store in the fridge for up to 7 days.

Makes 10
—
Prep 2 mins
—
Cook 2 mins

SCRAMBLED EGG AND BACON CROISSANT

Scrambled egg and bacon are revelations in the microwave, both yielding perfect results. Eggs come out soft and silky, and if you're a fan of crispy bacon, this recipe is for you. Cooking the bacon between sheets of paper towel also soaks up a lot of the fat, making this healthier than frying, too.

6 rashers of streaky bacon
4 eggs
2 tbsp milk
2 croissants, split in half lengthways
    horizontally
sea salt and freshly ground black
    pepper
small bunch of chives, finely chopped

Place four paper towels on a microwaveable plate, lay the bacon rashers on top then cover with two more sheets of paper. Microwave on high (800W) for 3–5 minutes, depending on how crispy you like your bacon.

Place the eggs and milk in a microwaveable bowl with some salt and pepper. Whisk together, then microwave for 2 minutes, stirring every 30 seconds. Microwave for a further 15 seconds for soft-set eggs or 30 seconds for a firmer scramble.

Fill the croissants with the scrambled egg and bacon and scatter over the chives.

Serves 2
–
Prep 2 mins
–
Cook 8 mins

BREAKFAST MUFFINS

A mug muffin couldn't be simpler, and it makes for a super-quick breakfast. Full of wholesome goodness and ready in under 5 minutes, it's perfect for a speedy start to the day.

6 tbsp wholemeal plain
  (all-purpose) flour
1 tsp baking powder
large pinch of ground cinnamon
2 eggs
2 small bananas, mashed
4 tsp maple syrup
80g (3oz) blueberries

Mix together the flour, baking powder and cinnamon in a bowl or jug (it doesn't need to be microwaveable). Whisk in the eggs followed by the bananas and maple syrup.

Fold through the blueberries then transfer to four large, microwave-safe mugs, or eight ramekins lined with paper cases. If using mugs, microwave two at a time on high (800W) for 3–3½ minutes until puffed up and cooked through, then repeat with the remaining two. If using ramekins, microwave four at a time for 2–3 minutes, until risen and springy to the touch.

Either eat straight from the mugs or ramekins, or turn the muffins out onto a plate.

**Makes 4 mugs or
8 paper cases**
–
Prep 3 mins
–
Cook 7 mins

SPINACH, HAM AND EGG BREAKFAST MUG

If you're a savoury breakfast person, this recipe is essentially a mug-shaped omelette. Ready in under 5 minutes, it will set you up for the day with very minimal effort.

large handful of spinach
2 eggs
1 tbsp milk
pinch of chilli flakes (optional)
1 slice of ham, roughly torn into pieces

Put the spinach into a large mug with a splash of water and microwave on high (800W) for 1 minute. Use a spoon to squeeze the spinach against the mug and pour out any excess water.

Add the eggs, milk, chilli, if using, and some seasoning to the mug and whisk everything together.

Add the ham and stir, then microwave on high for 2 minutes until puffed up and cooked through.

Serves 1
—
Prep 2 mins
—
Cook 3 mins

BERRY COMPOTE, YOGURT AND GRANOLA

A speedy way to make a compote, this recipe is perfect for the microwave. It can be made in advance and stored in the fridge.

200g (7oz) frozen mixed berries
200g (7oz) natural yogurt
2 tbsp granola
2 tsp honey

Put the berries and 1 tablespoon of water in a microwave-safe bowl and microwave on high (800W) for 1 minute.

Stir, then microwave for 5 minutes, until reduced and syrupy. Divide the yogurt between two bowls and top with the compote, granola and honey.

Serves 2
—
Prep 1 min
—
Cook 6 mins

EGGS BENEDICT

Poaching eggs in the microwave is very simple – you just need to make sure you follow the steps below to avoid any yolk explosions. I now have a dedicated egg piercing pin in my utensil drawer. With ham and a very easy hollandaise sauce, this is a classic brunch dish for a reason.

60g (2½oz) unsalted butter
4 eggs, plus 2 yolks
pinch of cayenne pepper
juice of ¼ lemon
2 English muffins, toasted
2 slices of ham, halved
sea salt

Melt the butter in a microwave-safe small bowl or jug on high (800W) for 30 seconds.

Whisk the egg yolks, cayenne pepper, lemon juice and a pinch of salt in a separate microwave-safe bowl or jug, then slowly pour in the melted butter and whisk to combine. Microwave on high for 15 seconds or until you have a thickened and glossy sauce.

Half-fill four small mugs with warm water from the tap, then crack an egg into each. Carefully pierce the yolk with a pin and microwave two at a time on high for 1–1½ minutes.

Check and microwave for a further 15–20 seconds, if needed, for a firmer yolk. Repeat with the remaining two eggs. Top each toasted muffin half with a piece of ham, drain the eggs using a slotted spoon and place them on top, then drizzle over the hollandaise sauce.

Serves 2
–
Prep 5 mins
–
Cook 5 mins

SAVOURY FRENCH TOAST WITH AVOCADO, FETA AND CHILLI

Although you won't quite achieve the crunchy golden crust from frying bread in butter, this version of French toast (or eggy bread in the UK) is healthier, quicker and tastes just as delicious. It's served Australian-brunch-style with smashed avo, tangy feta and a sprinkle of chilli flakes.

1 egg
1 tbsp milk
1 thick slice of bread
1 small avocado
1 tsp extra virgin olive oil, plus extra
    to serve
squeeze of lemon juice
pinch of chilli flakes, plus extra to serve
20g (¾oz) feta, crumbled
sea salt and freshly ground black
    pepper

Whisk the egg, milk and some salt and pepper in a shallow microwave-safe dish that fits your slice of bread. Dip the bread in the mixture, turning it until most of the egg is soaked up.

Mash the avocado with the olive oil, lemon juice, chilli flakes and some salt and pepper together in a bowl.

Put the dish with the bread in the microwave and microwave on high (800W) for 2 minutes, turning the bread over every 30 seconds. Transfer the bread to a plate, then top with the mashed avocado, feta, an extra sprinkle of chilli flakes and a drizzle of olive oil.

Serves 1
–
Prep 5 mins
–
Cook 2 mins

Breakfast

SNACKS

A microwave's ability to cook food quickly makes it the perfect appliance for a quick hunger fix or for when you have last-minute guests. In honour of the engineer who discovered microwave popcorn, I have included a recipe for a sweet, spicy and salty version, along with some other satisfying snacks that may surprise you.

SWEET, SALTY AND SPICY POPCORN

Popcorn was the very first food to be tested in a microwave, so naturally I had to include a recipe in this book. Cheaper and healthier than buying the pre-packed popping bags, making your own popcorn from scratch is the way to go. The combination of salt, sugar and spice used here works a treat.

60g (2¼oz) corn kernels
1 tsp olive oil
¼ tsp sea salt
¼ tsp hot smoked paprika
¼ tsp caster (superfine) sugar

Put the corn into a large microwave-safe pot with a lid that fits loosely – ideally glass or transparent plastic so that you can see through it.

Microwave on high (800W) for 1–3 minutes, then check to see the bottom of the pot for unpopped kernels. If there are lots, microwave for a further 30 seconds. Tip the popcorn into a large bowl and add the oil, salt, paprika and sugar. Mix well to coat the corn, then transfer to a serving bowl.

Serves 2
–
Prep 1 mins
–
Cook 2–3 mins

POPPADOMS, RAITA AND CHUTNEY

Eating poppadoms freshly popped from the microwave is a revelation – they come out crispy and, most importantly, warm. You can buy large packs of the uncooked discs from Indian supermarkets so it's a perfect store-cupboard hack, and will save you a fortune when you order a takeaway. Served with a cheat's mint yogurt raita and classic mango chutney – my favourite part of an Indian meal.

100g (3½oz) natural yogurt
5cm (2in) chunk of cucumber, diced
1 tsp mint sauce
1 tsp nigella seeds
4 uncooked poppadoms
4 tbsp mango chutney
sea salt and freshly ground black
   pepper

Put the yogurt, cucumber, mint sauce, most of the nigella seeds and some salt and pepper in a small bowl and mix together. Scatter the remaining nigella seeds over the top.

Line a microwave-safe plate with paper towel and microwave each poppadom on high (800W) for 30 seconds or until fully cooked and crispy. This may vary depending on your microwave. Serve the poppadoms with the raita and chutney.

Serves 2
–
Prep 2 mins
–
Cook 2 mins

PAPRIKA VEGETABLE CRISPS

Crisps (chips)? In a microwave? Yes, absolutely. The only downside is that you can't make a huge amount at once – but if you are craving a crunchy snack and have a potato or any other root vegetables lying around, it's so easy to make your own crisps.

500g (1lb 2oz) root vegetables, e.g. potato, sweet potato, beetroot, carrot, parsnip
1 tbsp olive oil
2 tsp smoked paprika
sea salt and freshly ground black pepper

Scrub the vegetables (no need to peel) and very thinly slice them, ideally using a mandolin. Transfer to a large bowl and mix with the olive oil, paprika and some seasoning.

Line a microwaveable plate with non-stick baking parchment. Working in batches, spread out some of the vegetable slices in a single layer, leaving a small space between them, then microwave on high (800W) for 3–5 minutes, flipping the slices and checking every minute to ensure they don't burn. Transfer to a board or plate to cool. Repeat until all the slices are used up – you will probably need to do this in at least four batches. Transfer to a bowl or platter and sprinkle with sea salt to serve.

Makes 1 small bowl
–
Prep 5 mins
–
Cook 12–20 mins

Snacks

NACHOS

Another crunchy snack I'm sure most people wouldn't have thought was possible in a microwave. Crisping up tortilla wraps to make your own nachos is incredibly quick and easy – just cover them with cheese, microwave for 30 seconds then add your favourite toppings and you're good to go.

2 tortilla wraps, cut into chip-sized triangles
100g (3½oz) grated cheese such as Monterey Jack
2 tbsp guacamole
2 tbsp sour cream
2 tbsp tomato salsa
2 tbsp pickled jalapeños

Put half the tortilla triangles on a microwave-safe plate and microwave on high (800W) for 30 seconds, then turn over and microwave for a further 10 seconds or until they have browned slightly.

Transfer to a plate to cool, then repeat with the remaining triangles. Once all the triangles are cool and have crisped up, pile them back onto a microwave-safe plate, scatter over the cheese and microwave for 15–30 seconds until fully melted.

Dot over the guacamole, sour cream, salsa and jalapeños to serve. Eat right away.

Serves 2
–
Prep 5 mins
–
Cook 1½ mins

BABA GANOUSH AND PITTA

Cooking aubergine in a microwave is a revelation I'm pleased to share. The flesh is rendered creamy and soft in a fraction of the time it would take to cook aubergine on the hob or in the oven. If you don't have a toaster, the pitta can easily be warmed in the microwave for 20–30 seconds.

1 large aubergine
1 small garlic clove, finely grated
juice of 1 lemon
1 tbsp extra virgin olive oil, plus extra
  to drizzle
1 tbsp tahini
pinch of smoked paprika
sea salt and freshly ground black
  pepper
2 toasted pitta, cut into triangles, to
  serve

Prick the aubergine all over using a fork and microwave on high (800W) for 8 minutes, turning halfway through, until it is completely soft. Leave to cool slightly then split it open, scoop the flesh out onto a board and finely chop.

Transfer to a bowl and mix with the garlic, lemon juice, oil, tahini and some seasoning. Drizzle over some more oil, sprinkle with paprika and serve with the toasted pitta.

Serves 2
–
Prep 2 mins
–
Cook 8 mins

MEAT

From tender shredded chicken tacos to tongue-tingling pork noodles, I've included lots of recipes for meat lovers to get excited about. The crispy onions were a revelation and go perfectly with the hot dogs but can also accompany so many other dishes, adding an irresistible umami crunch.

DAN DAN NOODLES

My take on this Szechuan noodle dish is spiced with tongue-tingling Szechuan peppercorns, five spice and fiery chilli oil, which all come together to produce a punchy, layered flavour.

2 × 150g (5½oz) packs of straight-to-wok udon noodles

200g (7oz) Tenderstem broccoli (broccolini), cut into 5cm (2in) pieces, thick stems halved lengthways

150g (5½oz) mushrooms, sliced

250g (9oz) minced (ground) pork

2 spring onions (scallions), white parts finely chopped, greens sliced

1 tsp Szechuan peppercorns, ground in a pestle and mortar

1 tsp five spice powder

2 tbsp soy sauce

1 tbsp hoisin sauce

1 tbsp Shaoxing rice wine

1 tsp garlic powder

3 tbsp tahini

½–1 tbsp chilli oil, to taste, plus extra to serve

¼ cucumber, coarsely grated or cut into matchsticks

Put the noodles into a large heatproof bowl and cover with boiling water.

Put the Tenderstem broccoli into a microwave-safe, lidded pot with a splash of water and microwave on high (800W) for 2½ minutes. Drain then put the lid back on to keep warm.

Place the mushrooms in another bowl and microwave uncovered on high for 3 minutes. Don't drain the liquid away and cover to keep warm.

In a separate microwave-safe bowl, mix the pork, white parts of the spring onions, ground Szechuan pepper, five spice, 1 tablespoon of the soy sauce, the hoisin, rice wine, garlic powder and some black pepper and microwave on high for 2 minutes. Stir then microwave for a further 1½ minutes or until the pork is cooked through.

In a small jug mix the remaining tablespoon of soy sauce, the tahini, chilli oil and 4 tablespoons of water from the mushrooms to make a loose sauce.

Drain the noodles and any remaining liquid from the mushrooms and add them to the large pot along with the broccoli, cooked pork and the tahini sauce. Mix really well and serve with the cucumber, green spring onion and a drizzle more chilli oil, if you like.

Serves 2

–

Prep 10 mins

–

Cook 9 mins

Meat

SHREDDED CHICKEN TACOS

Tender shredded chicken in 5 minutes? Absolutely. These super-quick tacos are stuffed with a delicious mix of creamy guacamole, juicy chicken, tangy feta and sharp pickled onions, all ready in just 10 minutes.

1 small red onion, finely sliced
1 lime, ½ juiced, ½ cut into wedges
2 chicken breasts
2 tsp fajita spice mix
2 tbsp barbecue sauce
1–2 tbsp mild Mexican hot sauce, to taste (I use Cholula)
6 small soft tacos/tortilla wraps
6 tbsp guacamole
100g (3½oz) feta cheese, crumbled
small handful of coriander (cilantro) leaves
sea salt and freshly ground black pepper

Mix the red onion, lime juice and some salt in a small bowl and leave to one side to pickle.

Flatten the chicken breasts to a thickness of 1–2cm (½–¾in). Place both pieces of chicken between large sheets of non-stick baking parchment, then pound with a rolling pin. Transfer the chicken to a shallow microwave-safe dish.

Scatter over the fajita spice mix and some salt and pepper, then pour in a small amount of water so that it comes halfway up the chicken. Loosely cover with cling film (plastic wrap) and microwave on high (800W) for 4–5 minutes, checking the centre and underneath to ensure the breasts are cooked through. When the chicken is cooked, the meat will be white and the juices will run clear.

Leave to stand for 1 minute then drain half of the liquid away, shred the chicken using two forks and stir in the barbecue and hot sauces. Cover and keep warm.

Warm the tacos in the microwave for 15 seconds, then spread each with a tablespoon of guacamole and top with the shredded chicken, red onion, crumbled feta and some coriander leaves. Serve with the lime wedges for squeezing over before eating.

Serves 2
–
Prep 5 mins
–
Cook 5 mins

Meat

CHORIZO, COURGETTE AND FETA ORZO

This winning combination of spicy chorizo, fresh mint and tangy feta works a treat with the soft, gentle background of quick-cook orzo and grated courgette (zucchini). This is a hearty, comforting meal, perfect for a quick weeknight dinner.

1 onion, finely chopped
2 garlic cloves, finely chopped
1 tbsp olive oil, plus a drizzle to serve
150g (5½oz) orzo
400ml (1¾ cups) hot chicken or vegetable stock
½ chorizo ring, about 100g (3½oz), chopped into 1–2cm (½–¾in) cubes
1 large courgette (zucchini), about 300g (10½oz), coarsely grated
small bunch of mint, leaves roughly chopped
100g (3½oz) feta, crumbled
sea salt and freshly ground black pepper

Put the onion, garlic, oil and a pinch of salt in small microwave-safe bowl and microwave on high (800W) for 3 minutes. Stir, then microwave for a further minute, until the onion is translucent.

Put the orzo and stock into a large microwave-safe bowl and microwave on high for 6–8 minutes, stirring every 2 minutes until the orzo is al dente. Drain and tip straight back into the bowl then add the onion and garlic, chorizo and courgette. Stir well then microwave for 3 minutes, stirring halfway, until the chorizo has started to release its oil.

Add most of the mint and feta and season with plenty of black pepper and a little salt, remembering that the feta is already salty. Serve topped with the remaining mint, feta and a drizzle of olive oil.

Serves 2
–
Prep 5 mins
–
Cook 15 mins

CHEAT'S CASSOULET

This classic French comfort dish takes hours to cook on the hob or in the oven but by using a few cheat's ingredients, you can have a warming bowl of pork and beans ready in around 20 minutes. Serve the cassoulet with crusty bread to mop up its delicious juices.

1 onion, finely chopped
2 garlic cloves, finely chopped
2 tbsp olive oil
100g (3½oz) bacon lardons
about 160g (5¾oz) smoked cooked sausage, sliced
1 × 400g (14oz) tin (can) cannellini beans
3½ tbsp chicken stock
1 tsp thyme leaves or dried thyme
1 tsp Dijon mustard
1 tsp white wine vinegar
2 large handfuls of green salad leaves
sea salt and freshly ground pepper
crusty bread, to serve

Put the onion, garlic, 1 tablespoon of the olive oil and a pinch of salt in a large microwave-safe bowl and microwave on high (800W) for 3 minutes. Stir in the lardons and microwave for 1 minute.

Add the smoked sausage and beans, including the liquid from the tin, the chicken stock, thyme and some salt and pepper and microwave on high for 12 minutes, stirring halfway through. The liquid should have reduced to form a sauce.

Whisk the remaining tablespoon of olive oil with the mustard, vinegar and some seasoning, then toss with the salad leaves and serve alongside the cassoulet with some crusty bread.

Serves 2
–
Prep 5 mins
–
Cook 16 mins

Meat

SPAGHETTI MEATBALLS

Juicy meatballs in a rich tomato sauce – my recipe for this classic crowd-pleaser is ready in just over 30 minutes. If you're cooking for one, the leftover meatballs and sauce can easily be frozen and saved for a speedy dinner another night.

150g (5½oz) spaghetti, snapped in half
4 tsp dried breadcrumbs
4 tsp milk
200g (7oz) minced (ground) beef
200g (7oz) minced (ground) pork
1 tsp garlic powder
1 tsp dried oregano
1 egg
1 onion, finely chopped
1 tbsp olive oil
350ml (1½ cups) passata
½ bunch basil, roughly chopped, reserving a few leaves
25g (1oz) Parmesan cheese, finely grated
sea salt and freshly ground pepper

Put the spaghetti into a large microwave-safe bowl with a big pinch of salt and cover with warm water from the tap. Loosely cover and microwave on high (800W) for 12–14 minutes or until al dente. Drain, reserving a mugful of the cooking water.

Meanwhile, soak the breadcrumbs in the milk in a large bowl then add the beef, pork, garlic granules, oregano, egg and some salt and pepper. Mix together really well then use your hands to form into 8 meatballs. Put these into a wide microwave-safe dish so that they fit in a single layer and refrigerate until needed.

Put the onion, olive oil and some salt in a large jug and microwave on high for 4 minutes or until soft. Pour in the passata and a big splash of the reserved pasta water. Season and microwave, uncovered, on high for 5 minutes, then stir in the chopped basil.

Microwave the meatballs on high for 4 minutes then drain off some of the liquid, turn the meatballs over and mix them so the ones in the centre are now around the edges, then microwave for another 2 minutes. Pour over the tomato sauce and cook for another 3 minutes. Scatter over most of the grated Parmesan and microwave for 1 more minute.

Tip the meatballs and sauce into the bowl of drained spaghetti, stirring well. Serve in bowls topped with the remaining Parmesan and the reserved basil leaves.

Serves 2
–
Prep 5 mins
–
Cook 33 mins

Meat

PARMA HAM, COURGETTE AND BASIL FRITTATA

You'll need a wide, shallow dish for this recipe – a ceramic pie dish would be ideal. Fresh and light, this frittata is very easy to make and is perfect for a quick lunch.

300g (10½oz) potatoes, sliced
spray of oil
200g (7oz) courgettes (zucchini),
    peeled into ribbons
4 slices of Parma ham, roughly torn
15g (½oz) basil, leaves picked
6 medium eggs
4 tbsp milk
30g (1¼oz) Parmesan cheese, finely
    grated

Put the potatoes into a lidded microwave pot with a splash of water and microwave on high (800W) for 4 minutes, then drain.

Spray a microwave-safe round, shallow dish (about 24cm/9½in) with oil and arrange the potatoes, courgette ribbons, ham and basil leaves in layers with plenty of salt and pepper. Whisk the eggs, milk, half the Parmesan and some black pepper in a jug, then pour the mixture over the dish.

Scatter over the remaining Parmesan and microwave on high for 10–12 minutes or until set in the middle.

Serves 3
–
Prep 5 mins
–
Cook 16 mins

PORK AND EGG-FRIED RICE

This microwave version of egg-fried rice uses sausagemeat and plenty of veggies for a simple weeknight dinner that's packed with flavour. Add as much chilli oil as you dare!

150g (5½oz) mushrooms, sliced
½ spring cabbage, finely sliced
3 sausages
2 spring onions (scallions), white part finely chopped, green part finely sliced
2 tbsp soy sauce
2 tbsp sesame oil
½–1 tbsp chilli oil, to taste, plus extra to serve
2 eggs
1 × 250g (9oz) pouch of microwave rice of your choice (I use basmati)
1 medium carrot, coarsely grated or julienned
freshly ground black pepper

Put the mushrooms into a large microwave-safe bowl and microwave on high (800W) for 3 minutes, drain then cover to keep warm.

Put the cabbage and a splash of water into a separate microwave-safe bowl, then cover and microwave on high for 2½ minutes. Drain, then tip into the bowl with the mushrooms and cover again to keep warm.

Squeeze the sausagemeat out of its skins, divide the meat into 1–2cm (½–¾in) nuggets and put these into the bowl you just used for the cabbage along with the spring onion whites, half the soy sauce, half the sesame oil, chilli oil to taste and some black pepper. Microwave on high for 2 minutes. Stir, then microwave for a further 1½ minutes or until no pink sausagemeat remains.

Whisk the eggs with 2 tablespoons of water in a microwave-safe bowl or jug and microwave on high for 2 minutes, stirring every 30 seconds until just scrambled.

Heat the rice according to the packet instructions then tip into the mushroom and cabbage bowl along with the cooked sausagemeat, eggs, carrots and the remaining soy sauce and sesame oil. Serve in bowls topped with the green spring onion slices and a drizzle more chilli oil, if you like.

Serves 2
–
Prep 5 mins
–
Cook 13 mins

Meat

HOT DOGS, CARAMELIZED ONIONS AND APPLE COLESLAW

It was an exciting discovery to learn that you can produce golden crispy onions in the microwave, and in a fraction of the time it would take on the hob. Everyone is amazed. Top these hot dogs with your favourite sauce and a pile of the onions for a delicious crunch.

1 onion, finely sliced
2 tsp olive oil
¼ small green cabbage, finely shredded
¼ small red cabbage, finely shredded
1 small eating apple, coarsely grated
1 tsp white wine vinegar
2 frankfurters
2 brioche hot dog buns
sea salt and freshly ground black pepper
mustard or ketchup, to serve

To make the caramelized onions, put the onion, 1 teaspoon of the olive oil and a pinch of salt in a microwave-safe bowl and microwave on high (800W) for 3 minutes. Stir, then microwave for 2 more minutes, until golden and crispy.

To make the coleslaw, put both types of cabbage, the apple, the remaining teaspoon of olive oil, the vinegar and some salt and pepper in a bowl.

Heat the frankfurters as per the packet instructions. Warm the hot dog buns in the microwave for 15 seconds then fill them with the frankfurters and top with the caramelized onions and sauce of your choice. Serve alongside the coleslaw.

Serves 2
–
Prep 5 mins
–
Cook 8 mins

Meat

54

TOMATO AND CHORIZO RICE

This tomato-rich rice is complemented by the smoky heat of chorizo and paprika. Cooking everything together ensures a deep flavour. Serve this with a crisp salad for a speedy dinner.

1 onion, finely chopped
2 garlic cloves, finely chopped
1 tbsp olive oil
½ chorizo ring, diced
150g (5½oz) paella rice
500ml (2 cups) passata
1 tsp smoked paprika
sea salt and freshly ground black pepper
finely chopped parsley or chives, to garnish
green salad, to serve

Put the onion, garlic, oil and some salt in a large microwave-safe bowl and microwave on high (800W) for 4 minutes. Add the chorizo and microwave for 1 minute.

Stir in the rice, passata, paprika, 200ml (scant 1 cup) of water and some seasoning, then cover and microwave on high for 15 minutes. Stir (be careful of steam when you lift the lid!) and microwave for 3 more minutes. Leave covered for 10 minutes then stir and check the rice is cooked through.

Garnish with some chopped parsley or chives and serve with a green salad on the side.

Serves 2
–
Prep 2 mins
–
Cook 23 mins,
plus resting time

MOROCCAN CHICKEN STEW

This stew is mildly spiced with a great store-cupboard addition, ras el hanout, and the bitter tang of whole lemon slices. With olives and apricots for a lovely balance of sweet and savoury flavours, I hope this is a dinner recipe you'll come back to time and time again.

2 tbsp flaked almonds
4 skinless, boneless chicken thighs
2 tsp ras el hanout spice mix
1 lemon, ½ juiced, ½ very thinly sliced
120g (4½oz) couscous
250ml (1 cup) hot chicken stock
1 onion, finely chopped
2 garlic cloves, finely chopped
1 tbsp olive oil
2 tbsp tomato purée (paste)
75g (3oz) pitted green olives, roughly chopped
6 dried apricots, finely sliced
½ x 400g (14oz) tin (can) of chickpeas, drained and rinsed
½ bunch of parsley or dill, roughly chopped
sea salt and freshly ground black pepper

Put the almonds onto a microwave-safe plate and microwave on high (800W) for 3 minutes, stirring halfway through.

Mix the chicken thighs with the ras el hanout, lemon juice and some salt and pepper in a microwave-safe bowl that fits the chicken snugly. Cover and microwave on high for 3 minutes then turn the chicken over and microwave for a further 2 minutes. Check the chicken is cooked all the way through – the juices should run clear when the thickest part is pierced with a knife. Microwave for a further minute if needed, then keep covered to keep warm.

Tip the couscous into a bowl, pour over 150ml (scant ⅔ cup) of the stock and cover with a plate.

Put the onion, garlic, lemon slices, olive oil and a pinch of salt into a large microwave-safe bowl and microwave on high for 5 minutes, stirring halfway through. Add the tomato purée, olives, apricots, chickpeas and the remaining 100ml (scant ½ cup) of stock, stir well and microwave for 3 minutes.

Slice the chicken and tip it into the bowl along with the cooking juices, stir well and heat everything on high for 1 minute.

Fluff up the couscous with a fork and stir through most of the chopped parsley or dill. Serve the chicken stew alongside the couscous and scatter over the remaining herbs and toasted almonds.

Serves 2
–
Prep 5 mins
–
Cook 18 mins

Meat

FISH

You might never cook a piece of fish any other way after trying the recipe for parcel-steamed salmon. Microwave risotto is also a revelation as you don't need to be as hands-on you do when cooking on the hob – try my recipe with juicy prawns (shrimp), cod and fresh herbs.

STEAMED HARISSA SALMON AND GREENS PARCEL

Preparing fish in this way yields perfectly cooked, soft fish, and the cooking juices provide a lovely sauce for the vegetables. What's more, there's no hint of a fishy smell left lingering in your kitchen. This recipe will work with any other piece of fish – cod or haddock, for example.

150g (5½oz) green vegetables, e.g. Tenderstem broccoli (broccolini), green beans, mangetout
100g (3½oz) cherry tomatoes, halved
1 salmon fillet
1 tsp harissa paste
juice of ½ lemon
½ tsp extra virgin olive oil
sea salt and freshly ground black pepper

Put the green vegetables and a splash of water in a microwaveable pot with a lid. Microwave on high (800W) for 2½ minutes or until tender. Drain then put the lid on to keep warm.

Put a piece of baking parchment – roughly the same size as a plate that will fit in your microwave – onto a plate and place the cherry tomatoes and salmon fillet in the centre. Spoon the harissa over the salmon then drizzle over the lemon juice and olive oil and add some salt and pepper. Crimp and fold the edges of the paper to enclose the fish and make a parcel.

Microwave on high for 3 minutes, then carefully open the paper and serve the fish, tomatoes and juices from the parcel on top of the vegetables.

Serves 1
–
Prep 2 mins
–
Cook 6 mins

RED THAI-STYLE PRAWN CURRY

Curry in a hurry? This one boasts a deliciously fragrant sauce alongside crunchy vegetables and juicy prawns (shrimp), all in under 20 minutes.

2 spring onions (scallions), finely sliced
thumb-sized piece of ginger, peeled
   and finely grated
1 garlic clove, finely grated
1 tbsp vegetable oil
2 tbsp Thai red curry paste
250ml (1 cup) coconut cream
3½ tbsp hot fish or vegetable stock
2 tbsp fish sauce
75g (3oz) baby corn, halved lengthways
100g (3½oz) mangetout, sliced
   lengthways
165g (5¾oz) raw king prawns (shrimp)
1 × 250g (9oz) pouch of microwave
   jasmine rice
1 lime, halved
small bunch of coriander (cilantro),
   roughly chopped

Put the spring onions, ginger, garlic and vegetable oil into a large microwave-safe bowl and microwave on high (800W) for 3 minutes, stirring halfway through.

Add the curry paste and microwave on high for 1 minute, then stir in the coconut cream, stock, fish sauce, baby corn and mangetout. Microwave on high for 8 minutes, or until the vegetables are tender, stirring halfway through. Add the prawns and microwave for a further 2 minutes, then stir well.

Heat the rice according to the packet instructions. Squeeze in the juice from half the lime and cut the remaining half into wedges. Serve the curry alongside the rice, with the coriander scattered on top and the lime wedges alongside.

Serves 2
–
Prep 5 mins
–
Cook 16 mins

Fish

PRAWN NOODLE SOUP

This lovely warming, spicy, broth-based soup is perfect for a quick lunch on a cold day. You can swap the suggested vegetables for anything you have to hand.

2 nests of flat rice noodles, about 100g (3½oz)

1 lemongrass stalk, outer layers removed, finely chopped

thumb-sized piece of ginger, finely grated

2 garlic cloves, finely grated

1 red chilli, finely chopped

2 tsp vegetable oil

500ml (2 cups) chicken stock

1 tbsp fish sauce

1 pak choi, cut lengthways into 8 wedges

100g (3½oz) sugar snaps, halved lengthways

100g (3½oz) baby chestnut mushrooms, quartered

165g (5¾oz) raw king prawns (shrimp)

1 lime, halved

small bunch of coriander (cilantro), roughly chopped

Cover the noodles with boiling water and leave to soak for 3 minutes. Drain and put to one side.

Put the lemongrass, ginger, garlic, chilli and vegetable oil into a large microwave-safe bowl and microwave on high (800W) for 2 minutes, stirring halfway through. Add the stock, fish sauce, pak choi, sugar snaps and mushrooms and microwave for 2 minutes. Stir in the prawns and microwave for a further 2 minutes.

Squeeze in the juice from half the lime and cut the other half into wedges. Run the noodles under warm water to separate them, then divide them between two large bowls and ladle over the soup. Serve the noodles scattered with coriander and the lime wedges on the side.

Serves 2
–
Prep 5 mins
–
Cook 6 mins

Fish

THAI-STYLE PRAWN OMELETTE

This fragrant omelette is great for a quick, light lunch for one. The classic Thai combination of sweet, sour, salty, spicy and umami is perfectly complemented by the fresh herbs; all this needs is a crisp salad to serve.

2 eggs
1 spring onion (scallion), white part finely chopped, green part finely sliced
2 tsp fish sauce
a few sprigs of coriander (cilantro), leaves picked, stalks finely chopped
½ red chilli, deseeded and finely chopped
½ tsp vegetable oil or some oil spray
handful of beansprouts
75g (3oz) cooked king prawns (shrimp)
2.5cm (1in) piece of cucumber, sliced
few lettuce leaves
1 tbsp sweet chilli sauce
few mint leaves
1 lime wedge

Whisk the eggs, the white part of the spring onion, fish sauce, coriander stalks, half of the chilli and 2 tablespoons of water in a jug.

Brush the oil onto a lipped microwaveable plate (or spray it) or a shallow, round microwaveable pot and pour in the egg mix. Microwave on high (800W) for 1 minute, stirring halfway through, then microwave for a further minute. Scatter over the beansprouts and prawns, then microwave for 1 minute more.

Transfer the omelette to a plate with the cucumber and lettuce leaves. Drizzle over the sweet chilli sauce and garnish with the remaining red chilli, coriander and mint leaves. Squeeze over the lime to serve.

Serves 1
–
Prep 5 mins
–
Cook 3 mins

COD AND PRAWN RISOTTO

A great recipe to have up your sleeve as it's much less hands-on than cooking a risotto on the hob and you still end up with delicious, creamy rice. The fresh herbs and lemon juice really bring this dish to life.

1 onion, finely chopped
2 garlic cloves, finely chopped
1 fennel bulb, finely chopped
1 tbsp olive oil
175g (6oz) risotto rice
600ml (2½ cups) hot fish or
    vegetable stock
about 260g (9⅓oz) cod, cut into
    8 chunks
165g (5¾oz) raw king prawns (shrimp)
100g (3½oz) frozen peas
½ bunch of tarragon, leaves stripped
    and roughly chopped
½ bunch of dill, roughly chopped
½ lemon, cut into wedges
sea salt and freshly ground black
    pepper

Put the onion, garlic, fennel, olive oil and some salt into a large microwave-safe bowl and microwave on high (800W) for 8 minutes, stirring twice.

Add the rice and a third of the stock. Stir well then cover and microwave on high for 8 minutes. Pour in another third of the stock, stir and microwave for 3 minutes.

Add the remaining stock, stir and microwave for a further 3–5 minutes, until al dente and creamy. Add the cod, prawns and peas and microwave on high for 2 minutes or until the fish is cooked through. Stir in the chopped herbs, check the seasoning and serve with the lemon wedges.

Serves 2
–
Prep 5 mins
–
Cook 26 mins

Fish

BAKED SWEET POTATOES WITH HOT SMOKED SALMON

Jacket (baked) potatoes are likely one of the foods most often cooked in a microwave, so I had to include at least one recipe in this book. I've paired the creamy sweet potato with salty, smoky salmon and a tangy yogurt sauce.

2 medium sweet potatoes
150g (5½oz) Greek yogurt
grated zest and juice of ½ lemon
1 tbsp capers, roughly chopped
small bunch of dill, roughly chopped
2 hot smoked salmon fillets, skin
    removed
sea salt and freshly ground black
    pepper

Prick the potatoes all over using a fork, then microwave on high (800W) for 10 minutes, turning them halfway through.

Mix the yogurt, lemon zest and juice, most of the capers and dill and some salt and pepper in a bowl.

Split the sweet potatoes down the middle, spoon over some of the yogurt, flake over the salmon then top with the remaining yogurt and scatter over the reserved capers and dill.

Serves 2
–
Prep 2 mins
–
Cook 10 mins

SMOKED SALMON AND KALE QUICHE

For this recipe you'll need a wide, shallow dish that fits in your microwave – a ceramic pie dish is perfect. This simple take on a quiche using breadcrumbs instead of pastry is perfect for a quick lunch served with a green salad on the side.

100g (3½oz) kale, leaves stripped and roughly chopped, stalks discarded
2 tbsp dried breadcrumbs
1 tsp dried mixed herbs
spray of oil
1 red onion, finely sliced
1 tbsp olive oil
100g (3½oz) smoked salmon, torn into pieces
5 medium eggs
3½ tbsp milk
pinch of chilli flakes
1 lemon, cut into wedges
sea salt and freshly ground black pepper
salad leaves, to serve

Put the kale into a large microwave-safe bowl with a big splash of water and microwave on high (800W) for 4 minutes, then drain.

Mix the breadcrumbs with the dried herbs. Spray a microwave-safe wide, shallow dish – about 24cm (9½in) in diameter – with the oil spray and scatter over the breadcrumb mixture to coat the bottom and sides of the dish.

Add the onion and olive oil to the bowl of kale and microwave for 3 minutes. Season, then tip the mixture into the breadcrumbed dish and spread it out in an even layer. Scatter over the smoked salmon so that it's evenly distributed.

Whisk the eggs, milk, chilli flakes and some seasoning in a jug then pour this into the dish.

Microwave on high for 8–10 minutes, or until the eggs have just set. Serve with salad and lemon wedges.

Serves 3–4
–
Prep 8 mins
–
Cook 17 mins

TUNA NIÇOISE SALAD

This combination of potatoes, eggs, tuna, crisp lettuce and a creamy sauce is a twist on a classic, served here with a sprinkle of crispy fried onions for an extra umami crunch. Cooking potatoes in the microwave is incredibly easy and if you follow the steps for boiling the eggs, you should avoid any explosions!

350g (12oz) new potatoes
2 medium eggs
1 tsp fine salt
75g (3oz) plain yogurt
¼ x 25g (1oz) pack of chives, finely chopped
2 anchovies, mashed with a fork
juice of ½ lemon
1 × 145g (5oz) tin (can) of tuna in spring water, drained
1 baby gem lettuce, leaves separated
2 tbsp crispy fried onions (shop-bought or see the recipe on page 54)

Put the potatoes into a microwave-safe pot with a lid. Add a splash of water, cover and microwave for 7 minutes or until you can easily pierce the flesh with the tip of a knife. Drain, then cut them in half.

Use a pin to pierce one end of each egg then put them in a microwave-safe jug or bowl. Cover with warm water from the tap so that it comes at least 5cm (2in) above the eggs. Stir in the teaspoon of salt and microwave for 4 minutes then leave to stand in the water for 6 minutes.

Drain the eggs and let them sit in cold water for a few minutes until cool enough to handle, then carefully peel and cut into quarters.

Meanwhile whisk the yogurt, most of the chives, the anchovies, lemon juice and some black pepper to make a dressing. Mix with the potatoes and tuna and stir to coat.

Divide the lettuce leaves between two bowls or plates, top with the potatoes and tuna, then add the eggs, the remaining chives and the crispy fried onions.

Serves 2
–
Prep 10 mins
–
Cook 11 mins
plus standing time

Fish

VEGGIE & VEGAN

Cooking vegetables is what most people already use their microwave for, but there are so many interesting dishes you might not have thought you could make. Try a mac and cheese that incorporates creamy cauliflower in the cheese sauce, a smoky bean chilli, mushroom enchiladas, an indulgent cacio e pepe spaghetti or some delicious pumpkin seed, spinach and feta muffins.

CAULIFLOWER MAC & CHEESE

The cheese sauce for this classic comfort dish has the addition of creamy cauliflower, giving it an earthy richness plus the added bonus of upping your vegetable intake.

½ cauliflower, about 300g (10½oz), roughly chopped
200ml (scant 1 cup) milk
150g (5½oz) mix of mozzarella and cheddar cheese, grated
1 tsp Dijon mustard
200g (7oz) dried macaroni
sea salt and freshly ground black pepper
green salad, to serve

Put the cauliflower, milk, 100ml (scant ½ cup) of water and some salt and pepper into a large microwave-safe bowl, loosely cover and microwave on high (800W) for 10 minutes, checking and stirring halfway through. Milk has a tendency to boil over, so make sure that the bowl is big enough and keep an eye on it.

Once the cauliflower is soft, blitz it with a stick blender until smooth. Add most of the cheese and the mustard and mix so that the cheese melts.

Put the macaroni into another large microwave-safe bowl and cover with 800ml (3½ cups) of water. Microwave on high for 6 minutes, stirring every 2 minutes.

Drain, then mix with the cauliflower sauce and tip into a shallow microwave-safe ceramic or glass dish. Scatter over the remaining cheese and microwave on high for 2 minutes. Serve with a green salad.

Serves 2
–
Prep 5 mins
–
Cook 18 mins

SMOKY BEAN CHILLI

This smoky, spicy chilli is packed with hearty vegetables and beans and makes use of shop-bought chipotle paste, which is a great store-cupboard product to have on hand. It's best served with rice, avocado, soured cream and some tortilla chips for dunking.

1 onion, finely chopped
2 garlic cloves, finely chopped
1 tbsp olive oil
1 sweet potato, about 250g (9oz),
    peeled and cut into 2cm (¾in) cubes
1 carrot, about 150g (5½oz), cut into
    2cm (¾in) cubes
1 tsp ground cumin
1–2 tbsp chipotle paste, to taste
200ml (scant 1 cup) passata
1 × 400g (14oz) tin (can) of black beans,
    drained and rinsed
1 × 400g (14oz) tin (can) of kidney
    beans, drained and rinsed
1 × 250g (9oz) pouch of microwave rice
1 small avocado, sliced
2 heaped tbsp soured cream
small bunch of coriander (cilantro),
    roughly chopped
sea salt and freshly ground black
    pepper

To serve
2 small handfuls of tortilla chips
½ lime, cut into wedges

Put the onion, garlic, oil and a pinch of salt into a large microwave-safe bowl and microwave on high (800W) for 3 minutes.

Add the sweet potato, carrot and ground cumin and microwave on high for 8 minutes, stirring halfway through. Stir in the chipotle paste, passata, beans, a splash of water and some seasoning and microwave for 4 minutes, stirring halfway through. Check that the sweet potatoes are tender enough for your liking and microwave for a little longer if necessary.

Heat the rice according to the packet instructions and serve on plates or in bowls with the chilli. Top with the avocado, soured cream and coriander. Serve the tortilla chips and lime wedges on the side.

Serves 2
–
Prep 5 mins
–
Cook 17 mins

Veggie & Vegan

RED LENTIL DAL

Dal is a perfect dish to make in the microwave; it soaks up all the flavours and stock as it cooks, as it would on the hob, yet the energy usage is lower. Topped with microwaved crispy onions and yogurt and served with bread for scooping it up, this is a lovely warming meal. Serve the dal on its own or as part of an Indian meal.

1 onion, finely sliced
2 tsp olive oil
2 garlic cloves, finely grated
thumb-sized piece of ginger, peeled and finely grated
1 tsp cumin seeds
1 tsp yellow mustard seeds
120g (4¼oz) red lentils
400ml (1¾ cups) vegetable stock
2 large tomatoes, about 150g (5½oz), finely chopped
1 tsp ground turmeric
1 tsp chilli powder
1 tsp ground coriander
small bunch of coriander (cilantro), roughly chopped
2 roti, chapati or paratha
4 tbsp plain yogurt
sea salt and freshly ground black pepper

Put the onion and half the olive oil into a small microwave-safe bowl and microwave on high (800W) for 5–6 minutes, checking and stirring every 30 seconds to 1 minute. Keep an eye on the bowl – the onions can burn easily – but if you keep checking and stirring, you should end up with crispy 'fried' onions.

Put the garlic, ginger, cumin seeds, mustard seeds and remaining oil into a separate small microwave-safe bowl and microwave for 1 minute 30 seconds, stirring every 30 seconds.

Put the lentils, stock, tomatoes and some salt and pepper into a large microwave-safe bowl, cover and microwave on high for 12 minutes, stirring halfway through. Stir in the turmeric, chilli powder and ground coriander. Continue to microwave uncovered for 6–7 minutes, stirring halfway through, until the lentils are cooked through and the liquid has reduced. Stir the garlic mixture and most of the chopped coriander into the lentils. Check that the seasoning is to your taste.

Warm the bread for 30 seconds and serve it alongside the dal, topped with the yogurt, crispy onions and the remaining chopped coriander.

Serves 2
–
Prep 5 mins
–
Cook 28 mins

TURKISH EGGS

This dish has become very popular recently and it's not hard to see why – it's pure comfort food: soft poached eggs surrounded by creamy, garlicky yogurt and drizzled with spiced butter. Serve it with plenty of toasted sourdough for scooping.

200g (7oz) Greek yogurt
1 small garlic clove, finely grated
juice of ½ lemon
2 tsp extra virgin olive oil
30g (1¼oz) salted butter
½ tsp Turkish chilli flakes
4 eggs
few sprigs of dill, roughly chopped
2 slices of sourdough bread, toasted
sea salt and freshly ground black pepper

Put the yogurt, garlic, lemon juice, half the oil and some seasoning into a small microwave-safe bowl and microwave on high (800W) for 1 minute, stirring halfway through.

Put the butter into a small microwave-safe bowl and microwave on high for 30 seconds. Swirl and microwave for a further 15 seconds, then add the chilli flakes and remaining oil.

Half-fill four small mugs with cold water then crack an egg into each one. Carefully pierce the yolks with a pin and microwave two mugs at a time on high for 1–1½ minutes, checking how firm they are after a minute. For a firmer yolk, cook for a further 15–20 seconds. Repeat with the remaining two mugs.

Divide the yogurt between two bowls. Use a slotted spoon to drain the eggs from the mugs and put them on top of the yogurt. Top with the chilli butter and dill and serve with the toast.

Serves 2
–
Prep 5 mins
–
Cook 5 mins

Veggie & Vegan

CACIO E PEPE SPAGHETTI

Cacio e pepe's creamy, glossy sauce is easy to create without your hob – you simply cook the pasta in the microwave then beat the cheese and crushed black pepper into the pasta's cooking water. Serve it with a bitter rocket salad to cut through the richness.

200g (7oz) spaghetti
100g (3½oz) pecorino, finely grated
25g (1oz) unsalted butter
1 tbsp olive oil
3 tsp black peppercorns, coarsely
    ground
2 handfuls of rocket leaves
1 tsp balsamic vinegar
sea salt and freshly ground black
    pepper

Snap the spaghetti in half and put it into a wide microwave-safe dish. Pour over 400ml (1¾ cups) of warm water from the tap, cover loosely and microwave on high (800W) for 8–10 minutes, stirring well every 2–3 minutes.

Add the pecorino, butter, olive oil and ground black pepper and beat rigorously until everything is combined and the spaghetti is coated in a glossy sauce, adding a splash of warm water if needed. Check that the seasoning is to your taste. Drizzle the balsamic vinegar over the rocket and serve alongside the spaghetti.

Serves 2
–
Prep 2 mins
–
Cook 11 mins

BUTTERNUT SQUASH AND HALLOUMI GRAIN SALAD

Cooking butternut squash in the microwave gives it a lovely soft and creamy texture, yet conversely you can also produce crispy kale. Halloumi, honey and chilli is a winning combination, delicious served with the vegetables and mixed grains in this healthy vegetarian main.

2 tbsp flaked almonds
½ butternut squash, about 700g (1lb 9oz), peeled, seeds removed and cut into 2cm (1in) chunks
1 tbsp, plus 1 tsp olive oil
2 large handfuls of kale, about 100g (3½oz), stalks removed and roughly torn
1 × 250g (9oz) pouch of mixed grains
220g (8oz) halloumi, cut into 8 slices
1 tsp runny honey
1 tsp Turkish chilli flakes
2 tbsp extra virgin olive oil
juice of ½ lemon
sea salt and freshly ground black pepper

Spread the almonds over a microwave-safe plate and microwave on high (800W) for 3 minutes, stirring halfway through.

Mix the butternut squash with the tablespoon of olive oil, some salt and pepper and a splash of water in a large microwave-safe bowl. Cover and microwave for 12 minutes, stirring every 3 minutes. Check the squash is soft and drain any excess water from the bowl.

Mix the kale with the teaspoon of olive oil and some salt and pepper, then spread half out on a large, microwave-safe plate and microwave for 3½ minutes on high. Check if the kale is crispy: if not, microwave for a further minute. Remove and repeat with the remaining kale.

Heat the grains according to the packet instructions.

Spread the halloumi slices out on a microwave-safe plate, drizzle over the honey and sprinkle on the chilli flakes then microwave for 1 minute 15 seconds, or until the halloumi has softened.

Add the kale, grains, extra virgin olive oil, lemon juice and any juices from the halloumi to the butternut squash and mix well. Serve in bowls topped with the halloumi and toasted almonds.

Serves 2

—

Prep 5 mins

—

Cook 23 mins

CHEESE, POTATO AND CHIVE SOUP

Luscious, cheesy potato soup is like a hug in a bowl, the perfect go-to on a cold day. Serve with crusty bread or buttery toast for dunking.

800g (1lb 12oz) potatoes, peeled and
    cut into 2cm (1in) cubes
1 onion, finely chopped
2 garlic cloves, finely chopped
1 litre (4 cups) hot vegetable stock
80g (3oz) cheddar cheese, grated
10g (½oz) chives, chopped
sea salt and freshly ground
    black pepper
crusty bread or buttered toast, to serve

Put the potatoes, onion, garlic, stock and some salt and pepper into a large microwave-safe bowl. Cover and microwave on high (800W) for 12 minutes, stirring halfway through, until the potatoes are soft.

Leave to stand for a few minutes, then use a stick blender to blitz until smooth (you may need to transfer the soup to a bigger vessel first to avoid any spillages or splashes).

Add most of the cheese and chives and stir until the cheese has melted. Check that the seasoning is to your taste, then ladle into two bowls and serve topped with the remaining cheese and chives. Serve the bread or toast on the side.

Serves 2
–
Prep 5 mins
–
Cook 12 mins

Veggie & Vegan

MUSHROOM ENCHILADAS

These smoky, spicy, mushroom-and-bean-filled enchiladas are cooked in a fraction of the time they would be in the oven. The stuffed tortillas are bathed in a chipotle tomato sauce and topped with cheese, crunchy crushed tortilla chips and piquant pickled jalapeños. Serve with soured cream to cool everything down.

1 onion, finely chopped
2 garlic cloves, finely chopped
1 tbsp olive oil
200g (7oz) baby button mushrooms, quartered
2 tsp fajita spice mix
400g (14oz) refried beans (they come in packets or tins/cans)
200g (7oz) passata
2 tsp chipotle paste
6 small tortilla wraps
100g (3½oz) grated cheese (I use cheddar)
handful of tortilla chips
2 tbsp pickled jalapeños, roughly chopped
small bunch of coriander (cilantro), roughly chopped
100g (3½oz) soured cream
sea salt and freshly ground black pepper

In a large microwave-safe bowl, microwave the onion, garlic, oil and a pinch of salt on high (800W) for 3 minutes.

Add the mushrooms and fajita spice mix and microwave on high for 6 minutes, stirring halfway through, then add the refried beans, stir well and microwave for a further 2 minutes. Check that the seasoning is to your taste. In a separate bowl, mix the passata with the chipotle paste and some seasoning.

Put a few spoonfuls of the tomato sauce in the bottom of a wide, shallow microwave-safe dish that will snugly fit the tortilla wraps after they've been filled and rolled.

Divide the mushroom mixture between the wraps, spooning a line of filling down the centre of each, then roll tightly and arrange in the dish. Spoon over the remaining tomato sauce, scatter over the cheese and microwave on high for 7 minutes or until the cheese is bubbling and the edges of the wraps have started to crisp up. Scrunch up the tortilla chips with your hands and scatter over the enchiladas, along with the jalapeños and coriander. Serve with the soured cream.

Serves 2
–
Prep 5 mins
–
Cook 18 mins

AUBERGINE AND EGG PITTA

Based on an Iraqi–Jewish recipe called sabich, this sandwich is stuffed full of finger-licking flavour. Soft yet crisp slices of aubergine, boiled eggs, hummus, tangy salad and vegetables are all piled into warmed pitta bread and topped with a tahini sauce and pickles. It's a messy but delicious affair.

2 eggs
1 aubergine, cut into 0.5cm (¼in) rounds
3 tsp olive oil
pinch of sumac
1 tbsp tahini
juice of ½ lemon
¼ cucumber, diced
6 cherry tomatoes, diced
½ tsp red wine vinegar
½ tsp pomegranate molasses
2 pitta breads
4 tbsp hummus
small wedge of cabbage, shredded
2 tbsp pickles
sea salt and freshly ground black pepper
small handful of parsley leaves, to serve

Carefully pierce the end of each egg with a pin. Put the eggs into a microwave-safe bowl or jug and cover with warm water from the tap so it reaches 5cm (2in) above the eggs. Add 1 teaspoon of salt to the water and microwave on high (800W) for 4 minutes, then leave to stand in the water for 6 minutes. Drain and cover with cold water until cool enough to handle, then peel and cut into quarters.

Put half the aubergine slices onto a microwave-safe plate and sprinkle with salt. Microwave on high for 2 minutes then turn over, sprinkle with salt and microwave for a further 2 minutes. Drizzle over 1 teaspoon of the oil and half the sumac, then microwave for a further 4–6 minutes, turning every 2 minutes, until the aubergine is cooked through and starting to crisp up. Repeat with the remaining aubergine, another teaspoon of oil and the remaining sumac.

Mix the tahini, lemon juice and a splash of water to make a smooth, loose sauce.

Mix the cucumber, tomatoes, the remaining teaspoon of oil, red wine vinegar, pomegranate molasses and some seasoning in a small bowl.

Warm the pitta in the microwave for 30 seconds then split open the pitta and fill them with the hummus, shredded cabbage, aubergine, cucumber and tomato salad, eggs and pickles. Drizzle over the tahini sauce and garnish with the parsley leaves.

Serves 2
–
Prep 10 mins
–
Cook 25 mins,
plus standing time

SPINACH, FETA AND PUMPKIN SEED MUG MUFFIN

A delicious, nutritious combination of spinach, tangy feta and crunchy pumpkin seeds makes this a perfect mid-afternoon or mid-morning snack, plus this recipe is so quick and easy you'll be rustling up fluffy mug muffins all the time.

1 tbsp pumpkin seeds
large handful of baby spinach leaves
3 tbsp plain (all-purpose) flour
½ tsp baking powder
1 egg
30g (1¼oz) feta
freshly ground black pepper

Spread the pumpkin seeds out on a microwaveable plate and microwave on high (800W) for 30 seconds. Stir, then microwave for a further 15 seconds.

Put the spinach into a large mug with a splash of water and microwave on high for 1 minute. Use a spoon to squeeze the spinach against the side of the mug, then pour out any excess water. Add the flour, baking powder, egg and some black pepper to the mug. Mix really well until no lumps of flour remain, then crumble in the feta and stir through the pumpkin seeds.

Microwave on high for 2½ minutes, until puffed up and cooked all the way through. Eat straight from the mug or tip out onto a plate.

Serves 1
—
Prep 2 mins
—
Cook 4 mins

Veggie & Vegan

SIDES

In writing this book, I discovered that the best vegetable to cook in the microwave is aubergine. Try my recipe for miso aubergine and you'll be amazed how soft and creamy the flesh becomes in such a short time. There are lots of options in this chapter for dishes to accompany all kinds of meals, from tahini creamed spinach and cheesy polenta, to honey-and-caraway-glazed carrots and spicy corn ribs that magically curl up during cooking and are a perfect side for a Mexican-style feast.

HONEY-AND-CARAWAY-GLAZED CARROTS

These sticky, sweet and lightly spiced carrots are ready in under 10 minutes. Caraway seeds add a mild aniseed flavour that works beautifully with the sweetness from the carrots.

300g (10½oz) carrots, peeled or
   scrubbed and thickly sliced
1 tbsp olive oil
1 tbsp honey
1 tsp caraway seeds
sea salt and freshly ground black
   pepper

Put the carrots, some salt and pepper and 1½ tablespoons of water in a microwave-safe dish, cover and microwave on high (800W) for 3 minutes.

Uncover and microwave for 2 minutes then stir in the oil, honey and caraway seeds and microwave for a further 3 minutes or until the carrots are cooked to your liking.

Serves 2
–
Prep 2
–
Cook 8 mins

SESAME MISO GREENS

You can use any green vegetables you like here, just check they're cooked to your liking before mixing them with the miso and sesame oil. These greens would be perfect alongside a juicy steak or stirred into rice noodles with some cooked prawns.

100g (3½oz) Tenderstem broccoli (broccolini)
¼ green cabbage, finely sliced
100g (3½oz) green beans
1 tbsp white miso paste
1 tbsp sesame oil
1 tsp sesame seeds

Put the broccoli, cabbage and green beans into a microwave-safe lidded pot with a splash of water and microwave on high (800W), loosely covered, for 3½ minutes, or until tender.

Mix the miso with 1 tablespoon of water, then add the sesame oil and mix again.

Drain the greens, then coat them in the sauce and scatter over the sesame seeds to serve.

Serves 2
–
Prep 1 min
–
Cook 3½ mins

TAHINI CREAMED SPINACH

This is an alternative take on the creamed spinach you may have had before, using tahini instead of cream. It goes really well with a pan-fried pork chop or a baked sweet potato (see page 72).

200g (7oz) baby spinach
2 tbsp tahini
1 tsp extra virgin olive oil
pinch of chilli flakes, to taste
sea salt and freshly ground black
   pepper

Put the spinach into a large microwave-safe bowl with a splash of water and microwave on high (800W) for 3 minutes, or until wilted. Tip into a colander and squeeze out as much excess water as possible.

Transfer to a bowl and mix with the tahini, olive oil, chilli and some seasoning.

Serves 2
–
Prep 2 mins
–
Cook 3 mins

Sides

POTATO AND PARMESAN GRATIN

Rich and unctuous, this gratin is a great side dish to serve with meat or fish and is so quick to make.

250ml (1 cup) double (heavy) cream
1 tsp cornflour (cornstarch)
1 tsp bouillon powder
½ tsp dried thyme
500g (1lb 2oz) potatoes, peeled and thinly sliced
20g (¾oz) Parmesan cheese, finely grated
sea salt and freshly ground black pepper

Whisk the double cream, cornflour, bouillon powder, thyme and some salt and pepper in a medium microwave-safe dish and microwave on high (800W) for 2 minutes, stirring halfway through.

Stir through the sliced potatoes and microwave on high, uncovered, for 10 minutes, or until you can easily pierce the potatoes with a sharp knife. Scatter over the parmesan and microwave for 1–2 minutes or until bubbling.

Serves 2
–
Prep 2 mins
–
Cook 14 mins

MISO AUBERGINE

Aubergine cooked in the microwave is so delicious; the flesh turns beautifully soft and creamy. Leaving it to marinate in the miso, soy and rice vinegar really amps up the flavour and leaves you with a deliciously umami dish that would go perfectly with some sticky rice or as part of an Asian meal.

1 aubergine
1 tbsp white miso paste
1 tbsp soy sauce
1 tbsp rice vinegar
1 tsp sesame seeds
1 spring onion (scallions), finely sliced
½ red chilli, finely sliced
sea salt and freshly ground black pepper

Cut the aubergine in half lengthways, then score a criss-cross pattern into the flesh, being careful not to cut through the skin, then cut each half in half lengthways again to make 4 wedges. Put these into a microwave-safe dish big enough to allow them to sit flat in a single layer.

Mix the miso, soy sauce, rice vinegar, 1 tablespoon of water and some black pepper in a small bowl, then pour the mixture over the aubergine, mixing well. Leave the aubergine to marinate, flesh-side down, for 10 minutes.

Cover the dish with cling film (pastic wrap) then microwave on high (800W) for 8 minutes. Carefully lift up the cling film (be careful of the steam) and turn the wedges over. Replace the cling film then microwave for a further 3 minutes or until soft all the way through.

Transfer to a serving dish and scatter over the sesame seeds, spring onion and chilli.

Serves 2
–
Prep 5 mins, plus marinating time
–
Cook 11 mins

CHIPOTLE CORN RIBS

Corn ribs are a great vegan or vegetarian alternative to traditional ribs. They are so easy to make, yet the way they magically curl makes them a really impressive dish. Take extra care when cutting through the whole cobs as they can be quite tough.

2 corn cobs
½–1 tsp chipotle powder, to taste
1 tsp olive oil
2 tbsp soured cream
juice of 1 lime
small handful of coriander (cilantro), roughly chopped
sea salt and freshly ground black pepper

Put the corn cobs onto a microwave-safe plate and microwave on high (800W) for 3 minutes.

Allow to cool slightly, then very carefully cut lengthways into quarters. I find the best way to do this is to stand the cobs up on their end and use a large knife to carefully slice downwards through the centre.

Put the corn, chipotle powder, oil and some salt and pepper into a large bowl and mix well to coat.

Return the corn to the plate and microwave on high for 4 minutes, turning halfway through, after which they should have curled up to look like ribs.

Mix the soured cream, lime juice and a pinch of salt and pepper in a small bowl, drizzle this over the corn ribs, then scatter over the coriander to serve.

Serves 2
–
Prep 5 mins
–
Cook 7 mins

BROCCOLI, CHILLI AND ALMONDS

This simple combination works really well and is a great way of jazzing up a fairly mundane vegetable. Toasting whole almonds in the microwave is another revelation – they get really crunchy and the process is much quicker than if you use the oven or hob.

2 tbsp whole almonds
small head of broccoli,
    about 200g (7oz)
1 tbsp extra virgin olive oil
grated zest and juice of ½ lemon
½ red chilli, finely sliced
sea salt and freshly ground black
    pepper

Put the almonds onto a microwaveable plate and microwave on high (800W) for 1–2 minutes, checking them after 1½ minutes. Transfer to a board and roughly chop.

Put the broccoli into a lidded, microwave-safe bowl with a splash of water and microwave on high for 2 minutes.

Drain the broccoli then add the olive oil, lemon zest and juice, chilli and some seasoning. Scatter over the chopped almonds to serve.

Serves 2
–
Prep 2 mins
–
Cook 4 mins

CHEESY POLENTA

This is a sure-fire crowd-pleaser – soft, silky and creamy. It's perfect served with slow-cooked stews or with sausages instead of mash. You can use any cheese you like or even mix two different types.

75g (3oz) quick-cook polenta
300ml (1¼ cups) vegetable stock
100ml (scant ½ cup) milk
50g (2oz) cheddar cheese, grated
sea salt and freshly ground black
    pepper

Put the polenta and stock into a large microwave-safe bowl and microwave on high (800W) for 5 minutes, stirring halfway through.

Stir well, then add the milk and microwave on high for 2 minutes, stirring halfway through. Add the cheese and stir to melt. Check the seasoning, adding salt as necessary, then grind over some black pepper to serve.

Serves 2
–
Prep 2 mins
–
Cook 7 mins

Sides

DESSERT

In this chapter you'll find desserts that take a fraction of the time they would in the oven, including a banana and miso crumble, a croissant bread and butter pudding and molten-middle chocolate pudding pots. The brownies come out just as they would if they'd been cooked in an oven – crumbly and fudgy in just 12 minutes, and there are some speedy meringues to have Eton mess ready in no time.

CORNFLAKE & RICE CRISPY SQUARES

This child-friendly (and let's face it, adult-friendly) treat is a combination of two recurring favourites: chocolate cornflake cakes and marshmallow rice crispy cakes. They're layered in a tin then cut into generous squares to produce absolute heaven.

150g (5½oz) unsalted butter
100g (3½oz) marshmallows
1 tbsp golden syrup (light treacle)
150g (5½oz) crisped rice cereal
250g (9oz) milk chocolate, broken into small pieces
large pinch of sea salt
100g (3½oz) cornflakes

Line a 30 × 20cm (12 × 8in) tray with baking parchment.

In a microwave-safe bowl, melt 75g (3oz) of the butter, the marshmallows and golden syrup on high (800W) for 1½ minutes in 30-second blasts, stirring after each blast. When everything is completely melted and combined, tip in the crisped rice and stir well to coat. Scrape the mixture into the lined tin and press into an even layer.

Put the remaining 75g (3oz) of butter into a microwave-safe bowl with the chocolate and microwave on high for 1½ minutes in 30-second blasts, stirring after each blast. Stir well and add the sea salt. Tip in the cornflakes and stir well again to coat. Use a spatula to scrape this mixture over the top of the rice crispy layer and spread it out evenly.

Place the tin in the fridge to set for at least 1 hour then cut into 12 squares.

Serves 12
–
Prep 5 mins
–
Cook 3 mins, plus setting time

ETON MESS

Who knew you could make crisp meringues in the microwave?! These require much less effort than traditional meringues, as there's no whipping to stiff peaks. Then you just have to let the meringues cool before smashing them up and combining them with vanilla-flecked cream, strawberries and shavings of white chocolate.

1 medium egg white
250g (9oz) icing (confectioner's) sugar
150ml (scant ⅔ cup) double
    (heavy) cream
½ tsp vanilla essence or bean paste
100g (3½oz) strawberries, sliced
20g (¾oz) white chocolate

Whisk the egg white until it's frothy, then sift in the icing sugar and beat until the mixture forms a thick paste.

Divide the mixture into 9 evenly-sized pieces and roll into balls. Place 3 balls on a piece of paper towel on a microwaveable plate, spaced apart. Microwave on high (800W) for 1 minute, watching as they puff up and take on a life of their own. Carefully remove the meringues from the microwave and repeat twice more with the remaining balls.

Whip the double cream and vanilla until you have soft peaks, then fold through the strawberries and crumble in one batch of three meringues.

Spoon into two bowls or glasses and grate or shave over the white chocolate to serve. Put the remaining meringues into an airtight container; they can be kept for around 5 days.

Serves 2, with meringue leftover

—

Prep 5 mins

—

Cook 3 mins

CHOCOLATE PUDDING POTS

These delicious, molten desserts need just over a minute's cooking – meaning you can rustle them up at the last minute (literally!). Serve the pots with a dollop of whipped cream and chocolate sprinkles, for nostalgia.

100ml (scant ½ cup) double (heavy) cream
60g (2¼oz) dark chocolate, chopped
60g (2¼oz) soft light brown sugar
60g (2¼oz) unsalted butter
50g (2oz) self-raising (self-rising) flour
1 medium egg
1 tbsp chocolate sprinkles
sea salt

Whip the double cream until it forms soft peaks.

Put the chocolate, sugar and butter into a microwave-safe bowl and microwave on high (800W) for 1 minute, stirring halfway through, or until everything has melted.

Fold in the flour and a pinch of salt, then add the egg and mix well to combine. Pour the mixture into two small microwave-safe mugs and microwave for 1 minute 15 seconds for a gooey centre. Serve topped with the whipped cream and chocolate sprinkles.

Serves 2
–
Prep 5 mins
–
Cook 2–3 mins

CHOCOLATE, BANANA AND MISO CRUMBLE

Underneath a crumbly, oaty top, the filling of this dessert is almost like chocolate banana cookie dough. It's perfect served with a big scoop of vanilla ice cream.

60g (2¼oz) unsalted butter, chilled and cut into cubes
1 tsp white miso paste
40g (1½oz) self-raising (self-rising) flour
70g (2½oz) golden caster (superfine) sugar
3 tbsp milk
40g (1½oz) milk chocolate chips
1 large banana, sliced
20g (¾oz) porridge oats
2 big scoops of vanilla ice cream, to serve

Melt 40g (1½oz) of the butter in a shallow, medium-sized microwave-safe dish (about 15cm/6in in diameter) on high (800W) for 30 seconds, then whisk in the miso, 30g (1¼oz) of the flour, 50g (2oz) of the sugar and the milk until fully combined. Fold in the chocolate chips then top with the banana slices.

Mix the remaining 20g (¾oz) of butter, 20g (¾oz) of sugar, 10g (½oz) of flour and the oats in a bowl and use your fingers to combine them and create a breadcrumb texture. Spread this over the bananas and microwave on high for 7 minutes. Leave to stand for 5 minutes then serve in bowls with a scoop of ice cream each.

Serves 2
–
Prep 5 mins
–
Cook 8 mins,
plus standing time

Dessert

SALTED CRUMBLY FUDGE

Making fudge on the hob is a laborious affair and requires lots of patience while you wait for the sugar to reach the perfect temperature. In the microwave, it takes just a bit of stirring and a fraction of the time. Ensure your bowl is very large: the sugar will rise up during cooking so you want to ensure it doesn't bubble over. And remember to take extra care when handling the bowl – it will be very hot!

400g (14oz) golden caster (superfine) sugar
1 × 397g (14oz) tin (can) of condensed milk
120g (4½oz) unsalted butter, cubed
1 tsp sea salt, plus extra to sprinkle

Line a 20cm (8in) square tin with baking parchment.

Put the caster sugar, condensed milk and butter into a very large microwave-safe glass bowl, mix well and microwave on high (800W) for a total of 12 minutes, stirring after 2 minutes using a wooden spoon or silicone spatula, then stirring again after each minute as it starts to bubble up. After the 12 minutes the mixture should be thickened and golden. Take care when removing the bowl from the microwave as it will be very hot.

Stir in the teaspoon of sea salt, then carefully pour the mixture into the lined tin and sprinkle with some more salt. Leave to set in a cool place for 1–2 hours, then cut into 36 squares.

Makes 36 squares
–
Prep 2 mins
–
Cook 12 mins

CHOCOLATE ORANGE SELF-SAUCING PUDDING

Simply pouring boiling water over the mixture before cooking encourages this pudding to magically produce its own rich chocolate sauce. With a zing of orange to complement the chocolate and a dollop of crème fraîche to cut through the richness, this is definitely a crowd-pleaser.

45g (1½oz) unsalted butter, cut into cubes
110ml (scant ½ cup) milk
100g (3½oz) caster (superfine) sugar
grated zest and juice of 1 orange
100g (3½oz) self-raising (self-rising) flour
30g (1¼oz) cocoa powder
50g (2oz) milk chocolate, roughly chopped
60g (2¼oz) soft brown sugar
crème fraiche or yogurt, to serve

Put the butter and milk into a microwave-safe glass or ceramic round or oval dish (15–20cm/6–8in) and microwave on high (800W) for 1 minute, stirring to melt the butter. Add the caster sugar, orange zest and juice and sift in all of the flour and half of the cocoa powder.

Mix well until fully combined then stir in the chocolate. Sift over the remaining cocoa powder, evenly sprinkle over the soft brown sugar, then carefully pour over 150ml (⅔ cup) of boiling water.

Microwave on high (800W) for 4–5 minutes, checking after 3 minutes in case the mixture is starting to bubble over. Leave to stand for at least 2 minutes before serving with crème fraîche or yogurt.

Serves 2–3
–
Prep 2 mins
–
Cook 6 mins, plus standing time

CHOCOLATE STEAMED PUDDING WITH SALTED CARAMEL SAUCE

Making steamed puddings on the hob can take hours so this is a very clever use of the microwave. The sauce is like liquid caramel and is a perfect pairing for the light, fluffy sponge. Drizzle with some extra cream if you fancy. Be careful not to overmix the batter as this can give the pudding a stodgy texture.

175g (6oz) unsalted butter, softened, plus extra for greasing
125g (4½oz) golden caster (superfine) sugar
2 medium eggs
4 tbsp milk
100g (3½oz) self-raising (self-rising) flour
25g (1oz) cocoa powder
50g (2oz) milk chocolate chips
100ml (scant ½ cup) double (heavy) cream, plus extra to serve
150g (5½oz) dark brown sugar
2 pinches of flaky sea salt

Liberally grease a 850ml (2-pint) microwave-safe pudding basin with butter and line the base with a disc of baking parchment. Beat 125g (4½oz) of the butter and the golden caster sugar together using a wooden spoon or spatula until pale and fluffy, then beat in the eggs, one by one.

Stir in the milk, then fold in the flour and cocoa powder until just combined, followed by the chocolate chips. Scrape the batter into the bowl and flatten the top. Cover with cling film (plastic wrap) and microwave on high (800W) for 3–4 minutes or until the centre is springy. Leave to stand while you make the sauce.

Put the remaining butter, the double cream and the dark brown sugar into a small microwave-safe bowl and microwave on high for 4 minutes, checking it every 30 seconds and stirring, stopping when it has thickened slightly and has turned golden in colour. The sauce will thicken as it cools, so be careful not to overcook it. Stir in the salt.

Carefully tip the pudding out onto a plate. Cut into 4 and serve with the caramel sauce and a drizzle of double cream, if you like.

Serves 4
–
Prep 5 mins
–
Cook 8 mins

Dessert

TRIPLE CHOCOLATE COOKIES

Here's something you probably never thought you could make in a microwave. These soft and chewy cookies are so quick to whip up and you can easily double the recipe and make two batches. Just be careful not to overwork the mixture.

40g (1½oz) unsalted butter
50g (2oz) soft brown sugar
2 tbsp milk
110g (4oz) plain (all-purpose) flour
¼ tsp baking powder
20g (¾oz) milk chocolate chips
20g (¾oz) white chocolate chips
20g (¾oz) dark chocolate chips
pinch of salt

Put the butter and sugar into a medium microwave-safe bowl and microwave on high (800W) for 30 seconds, stirring halfway through. Check that the butter has melted; if it hasn't, microwave for a few seconds more.

Mix in all the remaining ingredients and stir to combine, being very careful not to overwork the dough.

Line a microwaveable plate with baking parchment. Form the dough into 4 balls and put them on the plate, evenly spaced apart. Flatten each ball to approximately 8cm (3in) in diameter and microwave on high for 2½ minutes.

Remove from the microwave and leave to cool completely on a board or a cooling rack. The cookies will still be soft after cooking but will firm up as they cool.

Makes 4
–
Prep 5 mins
–
Cook 3 mins

GOLDEN SYRUP AND JAM CHEAT'S RICE PUDDING

This cheat's recipe uses pre-cooked rice – it's incredibly quick but tastes just like the real deal! There are endless options for toppings: berries, raisins, nuts or even just a grating of nutmeg. I've gone for a nostalgic version with strawberry jam (jelly) and golden syrup (light treacle).

1 × 250g (9oz) pouch of microwaveable jasmine rice
200ml (scant 1 cup) milk
½ tsp vanilla bean paste
2 tsp golden caster (superfine) sugar

To serve
2 tbsp strawberry jam (jelly)
2 tsp golden syrup (light treacle)

Put the rice, milk, vanilla and sugar into a large microwave-safe bowl and microwave on high (800W) for 5 minutes, stirring halfway through.

Eat straight away topped with the strawberry jam and a drizzle of golden syrup.

Serves 2
–
Prep 1 min
–
Cook 5 mins

Dessert

CARAMELIZED WHITE CHOCOLATE AND PECAN BROWNIES

You really can achieve the same results as oven-baked brownies with this recipe: a crisp top and a gooey centre. The difference? These are ready in just 5 minutes. Caramelized white chocolate adds a toasty sweetness and the pecans offer a contrasting crunch.

125g (4½oz) unsalted butter
150g (5½oz) golden caster (superfine) sugar
1 tsp vanilla bean paste
60g (2¼oz) cocoa powder
2 medium eggs
50g (2oz) plain (all-purpose) flour
100g caramelized (golden) white chocolate, roughly chopped
50g (2oz) pecans, roughly chopped

Put the butter into a microwave-safe rectangular dish (I used a 20 × 16cm/8 × 6in glass dish) and microwave on high (800W) for 1 minute, stirring halfway through.

Tip the melted butter into a bowl and brush what is left in the rectangular dish around the bottom and sides so that the dish is fully coated.

Add the sugar, vanilla and cocoa powder to the bowl and whisk together. Add the eggs one by one, whisking fully to incorporate each one, then fold in the flour.

Stir in the chocolate and pecans and scrape the mixture into the buttered dish. Microwave on high for 4–5 minutes, until the centre is just set. Leave to stand for at least 15 minutes before cutting into six squares.

Makes 6
–
Prep 5 mins
–
Cook 6 mins, plus standing time

CROISSANT BREAD AND BUTTER PUDDING

This is a great way to use up leftover croissants and you end up with the same results as you would if you cooked the pudding in the oven, but in only 5 minutes. You can swap the croissants for sliced bread or another type of leftover loaf, like panettone.

2 tbsp chocolate spread
2 butter croissants, thinly sliced
50g (2oz) dark chocolate chips
2 medium eggs
100ml (scant ½ cup) milk
½ tsp vanilla extract or vanilla bean paste
75g (3oz) golden caster (superfine) sugar
1 tsp demerara (raw brown) sugar

Spread the chocolate spread onto the croissant slices and arrange them in a medium, shallow microwave-safe dish that fits the slices snugly. Scatter over the chocolate chips.

Whisk the eggs, milk, vanilla and golden caster sugar together then pour the mixture over the croissants, pushing the slices down. Leave to stand for 15 minutes.

Sprinkle the demerara sugar over the pudding and microwave on high (800W) for 5 minutes or until the custard is just set. Leave to stand for 5 minutes before serving.

Serves 2
–
Prep 5 mins
–
Cook 5 mins, plus standing time

INDEX

ACKNOWLEDGEMENTS

A huge thank you to Stacey for commissioning me to write this book and to Alicia, Sofie and everyone else at Quadrille. Rita, it was a pleasure working with you; thank you for taking such beautiful photographs, and Max thank you for the gorgeous props.

A massive thank you to my army of assistants on set: Hattie, Sophie and Valeria, who most definitely picked up the slack when my heavily pregnant body needed to sit down!

And, of course, thank you to my chief recipe taster, my husband Aaron, who didn't tire of my hilarious question at every meal: 'Guess how *this* was cooked?'.